RELATIONSHIP NOT RELIGION

Put God First Both in Private and in Public

ADEOLA OKUBANJO

WESTBOW
PRESS
A DIVISION OF THOMAS NELSON
& ZONDERVAN

Copyright © 2014 Adeola Okubanjo.

All rights reserved. No part of this book may be used or reproduced by any means, graphic, electronic, or mechanical, including photocopying, recording, taping or by any information storage retrieval system without the written permission of the publisher except in the case of brief quotations embodied in critical articles and reviews.

Scriptures taken from the Holy Bible, New International Version®, NIV®. Copyright © 1973, 1978, 1984, 2011 by Biblica, Inc.™ Used by permission of Zondervan. All rights reserved worldwide. www.zondervan.com The "NIV" and "New International Version" are trademarks registered in the United States Patent and Trademark Office by Biblica, Inc.™

WestBow Press books may be ordered through booksellers or by contacting:

WestBow Press
A Division of Thomas Nelson & Zondervan
1663 Liberty Drive
Bloomington, IN 47403
www.westbowpress.com
1 (866) 928-1240

Because of the dynamic nature of the Internet, any web addresses or links contained in this book may have changed since publication and may no longer be valid. The views expressed in this work are solely those of the author and do not necessarily reflect the views of the publisher, and the publisher hereby disclaims any responsibility for them.

Any people depicted in stock imagery provided by Thinkstock are models, and such images are being used for illustrative purposes only. Certain stock imagery © Thinkstock.

ISBN: 978-1-4908-2001-9 (sc)
ISBN: 978-1-4908-2000-2 (hc)
ISBN: 978-1-4908-2002-6 (e)

Library of Congress Control Number: 2013922797

Printed in the United States of America.

WestBow Press rev. date: 04/03/2014

Contents

Preface xi

About the Author xv

Introduction xvii

Chapter 1: It's Not about You 1

Chapter 2: Change Your Ways 9

Chapter 3: Priorities 27

Chapter 4: The Change 39

Chapter 5: Comfort-Zone Christians 47

Chapter 6: The Call 55

Chapter 7: Struggling With Sin 65

Chapter 8: Not All Battles Are Physical 77

Chapter 9: Encouragement and Conclusion 85

The fear of the Lord *is the beginning of knowledge, but fools despise wisdom and discipline.*
—Proverbs 1:7

Dedication

Whoever speaks on their own does so to gain personal glory, but he who seeks the glory of the one who sent him is a man of truth; there is nothing false about him.
—John 7:18

For this reason, this book is dedicated to the one and only God almighty, the source of all wisdom, knowledge, and truth.

Exaltations

- God of peace
- God of love
- Merciful God
- God of hope
- God of Abraham
- The I Am That I Am
- The One who was, who is, and who will be forever
- The rose of Sharon
- The faithful God, though we are unfaithful
- The Eternal One
- The giver of life and opeHhope
- The all-knowing and ever-present God
- The ageless One
- Dependent on no one
- King above all kings
- God above all gods
- Unchanging God
- Unshakeable God
- God of Elijah

Preface

Writing this book has been somewhat of a battle. I kept getting prompts to be careful how I wrote it so as not to offend anyone. The truth is that whatever one does, one cannot please everybody. You will probably win some and alienate others. As Christians, however, we know that the Word of God (the Bible) is the absolute truth. It doesn't accommodate political correctness or cultural principles. It is the Word from the maker of all things, the source of all things. And yes, there are some things that may sound firm, but as a child of God, we cannot accept words that are sugar-coated or softened to appease our canal desires. The word must be told as it is. It is better to have the fear of God than the fear of man.

For the time will come when men will not put up with sound doctrine. Instead, to suit their own desires, they will gather around them a great number of

teachers to say what their itching ears want to hear. They will turn their ears away from the truth and turn aside to myths. But you, keep your head in all situations, endure hardship, do the work of an evangelist, discharge all the duties of your ministry.
—2 Timothy 4:3–5

Extracts from this book were first published in e-mails to a selected group of people. The extracts drew praises and criticisms alike. These extracts talked about some truths that are seldom taught in churches today, yet they are clearly illustrated in the Holy Bible. I was discouraged by negative comments, but the above passage lifted my spirit and gave me the confidence of the need to get this message out to God's people with the Holy Spirit doing the conviction of hearts.

In this age, with the ever-growing prominence of "liberalism" and "political correctness," the Word of God is fast being watered down to suit the changing taste of the world. I, therefore, feel compelled even more to get the Word of God delivered truthfully and undiluted. For this reason, the foundations of this book are firmly rooted in the Bible with constant references to the Word of God, which is alive, active, and 'sharper than any doubled-edge sword' (Hebrews 4:12).

Simply put, this book is designed to draw us closer to God, irrespective of where we are in our respective walk with Christ. I myself find sometimes, I just don't have enough time for God because I am so busy doing this and that. We seem to find time for everything else but God in our busy lives and squeeze God in here and there. Sometimes, we go the whole day without communicating with Him, but we remember Him and have all the time in the world when we are in desperate need. This should not be the case. I discovered that many times we are "convenient" children of God; seeking Him only when it suits us or need something from Him. But that's not right. It certainly isn't what God wants (i.e., us coming only when we need something from Him or performing self-righteous acts in front of man). He wants us to love Him and serve Him with all our heart and soul (Deuteronomy 11:13). This is achieved through a growing relationship with our maker. That growing relationship is paramount in a world where there are many pull factors (distractions) that are perishable and amount to nothing in the context of eternal life with Christ Jesus.

So I have been inspired to write this, firstly, to convict myself of the need to make necessary changes in my life and secondly to encourage my brothers and sisters in the Lord that our relationship with God is far more important than our religious acts. I hope everyone who reads this can take something positive out and be encouraged.

God bless.

About the Author

Adeola Okubanjo is a growing Christian with a passion for Christ. After relocating from London to a small town in the middle of England, he looked for a church to worship. On settling in one, he came to a realisation that what he was receiving from church was insufficient. For this reason, Adeola began to earnestly seek God's face and found there is great joy in getting to know God better.

In his quest, he discovered a number of things about God and why a personal relationship with God is of immense importance. One of his discoveries is that it's not about us but it is all about God. It's not all about what the church can give but what we can bring to the church.

His newfound relationship with God is enabling him to live a Christ-centred life both in and out of the comfort of the body of Christ. He hasn't arrived, but he has certainly left! The joy derived from knowing God personally enabled him to rededicate his life to Christ and engage in serving God, upholding the principles of Matthew 6:33.

He is currently serving in his local church in Nottinghamshire, England and practicing being a Christian outside of his "comfort zone" with the help of the Holy Spirit.

Adeola is blessed with a lovely wife, son and daughter.

Introduction

The purpose of this book is to draw all men closer to God, to encourage us to seek Him more through a personal relationship with Him. The principles of this book are firmly rooted in the Holy Bible (the Word of God). Hence, there is a continuous reference to the Bible because all authority comes from God the Creator (Romans 13:1)

I believe God's plan is to have a personal relationship with each of us where we commune continually with Him on a daily basis, evidence of which is all over the Scriptures. I have a relationship with my wife and speak to her countless number of times during the day. God seeks a similar type of relationship, where communication is not limited only to when we have a need or Sundays and is a two-way communication.

Why relationship and not religion?

Firstly, God's original plan was relationship. After God made everything and He saw that it was beautiful, He said, "*Let us make man in our image*" (Genesis 1:26). He made us with similar characteristics as Himself and Jesus so we can relate, commune, forge a sustainable relationship and ultimately serve Him. The first of the Ten Commandments encourages us to love God with all of our heart and soul. Even after Jesus came and summarised the commandments, loving God was still first. He didn't say, "Love your wife then me" or "Love your job then me." Deuteronomy chapter 11 emphasises further, the importance God attaches to a personal relationship with Himself.

> *So if you faithfully obey the commands I am giving you today—to love the Lord your God and to serve him with all your heart and with all your soul then I will send rain on your land in its season.*
> —Deuteronomy 11:13

In the Garden of Eden, God would come down during the "cool of the day" and commune with man (Genesis 3:8). Love should underpin our relationship with God, but as a result of disobedience; eating from the Tree of Knowledge of Good and Evil, man has been burdened with worries and problems, which seems to be the focal point of man's relationship with God, if any. These worries and burdens include, but are not limited to, *childbearing pains* (Genesis

3:16), *painful toil* (Genesis 3:17), and eventually *death* (Genesis 3:19).

Today, we have all sorts of worries to contend with, such as: food, clothing, shelter, jobs, the recession, security, safety, our children, family members, bills, health and more. Many people are been weighed down under these burdens and slip into depression. A lot more are struggling to make ends meet; most are living lives filled with stress. But Jesus came to give us life (John 3:16), life eternal, life to the fullest, life free from burdens, life with peace that surpasses human comprehension. This was further emphasised in Matthew 6:25–34, where the Bible encourages us not to worry about life but focus on Him and everything will be okay.

Secondly, "The God who made the world and everything in it is the Lord of heaven and earth and does not live in temples built by hands" (Acts 17:24). But He lives in our hearts. As a new or young Christian unsure which way to go, you are heavily dependent on hearing from God through the church and mature Christians. As you develop in your walk with Christ, your primary source for receiving from God should be directly from Him—a personal relationship with God—with the church providing a support base for your Christian walk. Going to church every Sunday and midweek programs does not guarantee eternal life. Drawing nearer to God, obeying His commandments and living a godly life on a daily basis will go further in securing eternity with Christ. A personal relationship with Christ does not discount the value of church, Bible studies, Christian conventions, etc. But it is an opportunity to build upon what is learned from these avenues and seek ways to apply them to your daily living.

Thirdly, religion is susceptible to the selfish ambitions and desires of man while a growing relationship with God is on a solid foundation. Over the years, man has used religion as a means to personal gain, twisted the word of God and manipulated the children of God, by exploiting his position of authority. This still occurs in our society today and for this reason, we need a personal relationship with God to discern the "wolf in a sheep's clothing". In other words, Christ is pure and should be a permanent fixture in our lives with a growing influence.

An inadequate relationship with God is the root cause of a lack of spiritual growth in many Christians and churches today. There are many Christians that have been saved for five, ten or twenty years but don't know how to pray, are incapable of reading the Bible without a guide, or take every decision to their pastor (when they could seek the face of God directly sometimes). A lot are still stuck on elementary things. Can you imagine a full-grown adult struggling to understand basic counting (one to ten) despite being in school for eleven years or more? This is unfortunately true about many Christians, because some of us haven't really grown spiritually due to the focus on religion at the expense of a relationship with God.

After Jesus comes back and takes his own, it wouldn't matter if one was Catholic, Anglican, Pentecostal, Methodist, Baptist, or any other denomination. So, why do we focus so much on religion and methodology with so little emphasis is given to a personal relationship with God?

Over the next few chapters, we will explore in great detail why our relationship with the Almighty is of significant importance. We will also identify the main obstacles (hindrances) in developing our relationships and how we can overcome them through the help of the Holy Spirit of God.

> *Seek the LORD while he may be found;*
> *call on him while he is near.*
> —Isaiah 55:6

> *Here I am! I stand at the door and knock. If anyone hears my voice and opens the door, I will come in and eat with him, and he with me.*
> —Revelation 3:20

> *Remember, therefore, what you have received and heard; obey it, and repent. But if you do not wake up, I will come like a thief, and you will not know at what time I will come to you.*
> —Revelation 3:3

Chapter 1

It's Not about You

This is what the L‍ord says—your Redeemer, the Holy One of Israel: "I am the L‍ord your God, who teaches you what is best for you, who directs you in the way you should go. If only you had paid attention to my commands, your peace would have been like a river, your righteousness like the waves of the sea."
—Isaiah 48:17–18

It is in our personal relationships with our maker that we fully understand that it's not about us but all about Him. We learn about God's plan for us and can confirm (or refute) what others have prophesied about us. The quicker we realize this, the easier life becomes. Now, when we talk about life becoming easier, we mean peace that passes human understanding even when we are going through "the valley of the shadow of death" because we know we have God's presence with us at all times. Being a Christian does not immune us from trouble or trials. Knowing God and having complete trust in Him give us the assurance that we will overcome when trials and tribulations come; with the Holy Spirit navigating us safely through. Therefore, we are at peace and relaxed because all is well. Peace like a river and joy like a fountain are benefits of a close and growing personal relationship with God because through Him, our confidence grows exponentially (Joshua 1:9).

All the earthly things we rate as important today will not matter on the last day. I've heard this statement made numerous times: "If you want to make God laugh, tell Him your plans." I subscribe to this statement. Pause and ask yourself how many plans you've made in the past and how many of them actually worked out exactly the way you envisaged.

> *Now Listen, you who say, "Today or tomorrow we will go to this or that city, and spend a year there, carry on business and make money." Why, you do not even know what will happen tomorrow. What is your life? You are a mist that appears for a little while and then vanishes. Instead, you ought to say, "If it is the Lord's will, we will live and do this or that."*
> James 4:13–15

Your life as you know it is for a very limited time compared to eternity. What you do in life counts as you will give an account of it (Matthew 25:31–46). According to this passage in Matthew, all of us will be separated in two groups, based on how we spent our lives. The analogy of sheep and goats is used here, but I am sure most people would prefer to be on the sheep's side.

A lot of us think we have time on our side and make excuses, such as *I am just starting my career so am too busy to do the will of God. I have kids. I am married. When I become a priest or pastor ... When I retire ...* And many more excuses. But God is the Creator. He gives life, takes it away, and is answerable to none (Job 1:21). People die every day, and there is no certainty that any of us will live to a certain age. I heard of a lady who recently finished medical school, had no health concerns, but died shortly after qualifying as a doctor in her mid twenties. Remember the parable of the rich fool in Luke 12:13–21? He looked at the wealth he amassed, loved it and planned to demolish the old barn in order to build a new one to accommodate the overflowing store of grain. His next move was to take life easy and enjoy, not knowing death was around the corner.

In a similar scenario, my former colleague's father-in-law had paid into a number of pensions. The man was extremely disciplined with money and 'preached' to all his children about the importance of saving and having a good pension. He overpaid into all his pension pots and lived a moderate lifestyle. Unfortunately, he died just before retirement so was unable to enjoy all his hard work and planning.

> *For a man may do his work with wisdom, knowledge
> and skill, and then he must leave all he owns
> to someone who has not worked for it. This too
> is meaningless and a great misfortune.*
> —Ecclesiastes 2:21

Two lessons can be derived from the above stories. Firstly, the Bible encourages us not to store up riches here on earth but in heaven (Matthew 6:19–20). Now this appears difficult to comprehend, as many of us have been brought up with the notion that we should save and store up assets to have a good retirement. But the Bible teaches us otherwise. We are to store up riches in heaven. But how do we store up riches in heaven? By giving up our earthly desires and living for Christ. Two of the biggest models of the New Testament, Jesus and Paul, didn't go about storing up treasure here on earth. In fact, I believe both of them did not have a regular salary but put Matthew 6:33 at the heart of their living and God provided the rest.

Secondly, God owns life. He decides who lives, who dies and when we die. He owns all and until we fully recognize this, life will continually be like running through head wind even if it seems like we are making progress.

> *You have planted much, but have harvested little. You
> eat but never, have enough. You drink, but never have*

your fill. You put on clothes, but are not warm. You earn wages, only to put them in a purse with holes in it.
—Haggai 1:6

*"You expected much, but see, it turn out to be little. What you brought home, I blew away. Why?" declares the L*ORD *Almighty. "Because of my house, which remains a ruin, while each of you is busy with his own house."*
—Haggai 1:9

How many people are struggling to make ends meet? You work hard but don't have enough, you earn money yet accumulate more debt, you become more successful in your career, but you are unhappy. This passage in Haggai is true of many because they've left God in the "back seat" while chasing those elusive targets, dreams, and goals that will bring "happiness." Haggai 1:9 emphasises that a lot of Christians have left the house of God in ruin while they build their own houses; this is why it appears people keep running into head wind. So the next logical question is this: how do we rebuild the house of the Lord that lies in ruins?

To do this, we must first identify what the house of the Lord is. The Bible says in 1 Corinthians 6:19–20 that our bodies are the temple of the Holy Spirit of God Himself, yet we subject our bodies to all sorts of sin and rubbish, up to the point that we have reconditioned our bodies to view some sins and things of this world as "acceptable."

> *Therefore, I urge you brothers, in view of God's mercy, to offer your bodies as living sacrifices, holy and pleasing to God.*
> —Romans 12:1

How can we offer a body contaminated with sin as a sacrifice to the Lord God almighty? In Old Testament terms, that would probably be like offering a disabled goat that is blind in both eyes to God as a sacrifice.

✪

In every creation, there is some sort of craving that has been engineered into the DNA. We seek to meet this longing through many avenues that ultimately fail to satisfy. We often think we would be happy if we achieve a certain level of wealth, career aspiration, or any other goals we set ourselves. Sometimes we attempt to fill this hole (craving) with sex, alcohol, fame, power, "spiritual enlightenment" and other sub-optimal desires. But the absolute truth is that only God can truly satisfy. Until you come to this impeccable simple understanding, you will achieve all the goals set but still find something lacking in your life.

> *Then Jesus declared, "I am the bread of life. He who comes to me will never go hungry, and he who believes in me will never be thirsty."*
> —John 6:35

Relationship not Religion

> *Why spend money on what is not bread, and your labour on what does not satisfy? Listen, listen to me, and eat what is good, and your soul will delight in the richest of fare.*
> —Isaiah 55:2

> *Jesus replied, "If anyone loves me, He will obey my teaching. My Father will love him, and we will come to him and make our home with him."*
> —John 14:23

Our relationship with God is the only remedy for the yearning (craving) that man has. A mind set on fleshly desires will find this impossible to comprehend until it tries everything, fails and discovers there is still something missing. We can save ourselves a whole lot of time, heartache, disappointments, and more if only we would choose to seek God diligently. He is waiting for you, knocking at your door, and ready to dine with you.

> *Take my yoke upon you and learn from me, for I am gentle and humble in heart, and you will find rest for your souls*
> —Matthew 11:29

✪

I have often looked at oppression and some other practices that go on in the world, and I get upset and think about how I can make a difference. We can make a difference by supporting the poor, standing up for what is right in the eyes of God and loving our neighbours as ourselves, irrespective of who they are and where they are from. Another way we can change the world is to bring forward the ending of this world in its present form. We do this by acting upon Matthew 24:14. In this passage, the disciples want to know when the world will end. Today many would love to know when the world would end so they can make necessary preparations. Jesus, however, gave the clearest hint of when this will happen and how to bring the end forward. He said when the gospel of the kingdom has been preached in the world as a testimony to all nations, the end will come. Indeed, our priorities (as identified in Matthew 6:33 and Matthew 28:19) should be telling the world about Christ. This is how we change our world permanently, bringing forward the second coming of Christ. As members of the body of Christ, we should gear our collective efforts toward ensuring that everyone in every corner of the earth has heard about Christ.

It's not about you or me, but it's all about God!

Submit yourselves, then, to God. Resist the devil, and he will flee from you. Come near to God and he will come near to you. Wash your hands, you sinners, and purify your hearts, you double-minded.
—James 4:7–8

Chapter 2

Change Your Ways

*He whose walk is upright fears the L*ORD*, but he whose ways are devious despises him.*
—Proverbs 14:2

The Bible stipulates that the righteousness of man is like filthy rags. A lot of us were brought up under the notion that we can earn eternal life by being religious; we believe going to church every Sunday, attending midweek services, serving in the church and other such activities will mitigate all forms of sin (those we engage in knowingly and unknowingly). We have even declassified some sins and placed higher emphasis on others. For example, the Bible condemns homosexuality, but breaking the speed limit while driving is not seen by many as sin. Neither is telling a "little white lie" or calling the name of Jesus or God in vain regarded as unacceptable before God. Many men will look at a woman, have lustful thoughts, albeit for a moment and think they haven't committed any sin since they did not have physical intercourse with her. But Matthew 5 says different.

But I tell you that anyone who looks at a woman lustfully has already committed adultery with her in his heart.
—Matthew 5:28

We sit down with friends and family and condemn leaders, politicians, pastors, and celebrities, but the Word of God says;

Do not judge, or you too will be judged.
—Matthew 7:1

Having a discussion on how useless a politician is or how sinful a celebrity is, reflects disobedience to the Word of God, which is a sin. Stop it!

Breaking the speed limit or doing anything contrary to the law of the land we live in is wrong, according to Romans 13:1–2.

Everyone must submit himself to the governing authorities, for there is no authority except that which God has established. The authorities that exist have been established by God. Consequently, he who rebels against the authority is rebelling against what God has instituted, and those who do so will bring judgment on themselves.

Tax is another "on-the-fence" issue, but with God, there is only right or wrong. Some think it is okay to evade taxation, but for Christians, this is not right. Many Christians and non-Christians running small, unregistered businesses feel that the burden of taxation is heavy or taxes are being spent unjustly. What does the Bible say on this matter? In Matthew 17:24–27, Jesus led by example in paying His taxes. He did not come up with excuses like "Oh, I travel a lot and am not resident" or "I don't like the way the government spends our money." He paid his tax promptly.

> *Give everyone what you owe him: If*
> *you owe taxes, pay taxes; …*
> —Romans 13:7

Jesus said:

> *Then give to Caesar what is Caesar's*
> *and to God what is God's.*
> -Luke 20:25

It is not right to owe people endlessly, especially when we have the means to pay it. The Bible encourages us to let no debt remain outstanding among us, but the debt of love. You could be blocking your blessings by choosing to ignore your debt obligations.

> *Let no debt remain outstanding, except the continuing debt to love one another, for he who loves his fellow-man has fulfilled the law.*
> —Romans 13:8

A solid and consistent personal relationship with God enhances the prominence of our God-given conscience. Our conscience convicts us when we are about to do the wrong thing. The more we get intoxicated with the world, the more we diminish the impact of our conscience.

> *The Lord says: "These people come near to me with their mouth and honour me with their lips, but their hearts are far from me. Their worship of me is made up only of rules taught by men."*
> —Isaiah 29:13

God sees everything (Jeremiah 23:24). There is certainly nothing hidden from the God, whose footstool is the earth (Acts 7:49). If you say you are a Christian and engage in adultery, fornication, give bribes, lie, steal, cheat and exercise envy, greed, or jealousy, how are you being good ambassadors of Christ?

> *You have seen many things, but have paid no attention; your ears are open, but you hear nothing.*
> —Isaiah 42:20

We must be careful not to fall into the trap of thinking we are "safe," because we are born again Christians, or have the grace of God, hence we can persist in our old ways.

> *When such a person hears the words of this oath, he invokes a blessing on himself and therefore thinks, "I will be safe even, though I persist in going my own way." This will bring disaster on the watered land as well as the dry. The LORD will never be willing to forgive him; his wrath and zeal will burn against that man. All the curses written in this book will fall upon him, and the LORD will blot out his name from under heaven.*
> —Deuteronomy 29:19–20

Our goal should be to seek to live a more godly life on a daily basis. Of course, we will make mistakes along the way, but we should continually seek to improve on the previous day with the help of the Holy Spirit and not persist in sinful ways.

> *I can do everything through him who gives me strength.*
> —Philippians 4:13

We must stop trying to fit into this world. Just because everyone is doing it (even other Christians) doesn't make it right. We are called to be a light in this darkened world.

> *If you belonged to the world, it would love you as its own. As it is, you do not belong to the world, but I have chosen you out of the world. That is why the world hates you.*
> —John 15:19

We don't need to gain man's approval by indulging in what is unacceptable to our heavenly Father. God is greater than man, so we should aim to please God over man.

> *Do not love the world or anything in the world. If anyone loves the world, the love of the father is not in him. For everything in the world—the cravings of a sinful man, the lust of his eyes and boasting of what he has and does comes - not from the Father but from the world. The world and its desires pass away, but the man who does the will of God lives forever.*
> —1 John 2:15–17

This world in its present form is not our home. Therefore we must not love the world as all will be destroyed and made new. Our reward is in heaven, but we find it difficult adhering to the passage above because of the many distractions and cravings readily available. Saying no the love of this world is a challenge that is achievable through the help of the Holy Spirit.

We must beware of making a similar mistake to Saul, which cost him his position. He went against God's will twice by choosing to please man over clear instructions from God. He thought sacrifice would cancel out disobedience but was wrong.

> *But Samuel replied: Does the LORD delight in burnt offerings and sacrifices as much as in obeying the*

voice of the L*ORD*? *To obey is better than sacrifice, and to heed is better than the fat of rams.*
—1 Samuel 15.22

We certainly cannot bribe our way into heaven with big, fat offerings, tithes, serving in church etc. while we indulge in disobedient activities. There is no sacrifice big enough to mitigate disobedience to God Almighty. The Jews missed it during the time Jesus was here on earth. They thought by engaging in religious acts, they would secure eternal life (Pharisees and Sadducees). Today, there is a widespread belief among some Christians of attaining eternal life by engaging in religious activities. This is sometimes interpreted as a "legalistic" approach to Christianity where a person engages in religious acts, based on self-righteousness. This approach also encourages (directly and indirectly) the condemnation of "sinners". The condemnation of "sinners" like prostitutes, drug addicts, convicts, single-mothers, homosexuals, criminals and others; results in disassociation with this group of people. However, a close examination of the Holy Book illustrates Jesus, hanging out with these "sinners" (Matthew 9:10, Matthew 15:21-28, John 4:1-26). Often we judge our fellow brothers and sisters who are in need of help and refuse to associate with them. But Jesus showed us the way by praying for them, encouraging them, and offering salvation. The same measure of love we display to those we hold dear should be shown to the unloved. We are not called to conditionally love our neighbours, but to love them as ourselves. Jesus showed unreserved love to us by rescuing us from our sinful ways (not because we are special). We asked to replicate this love to all men freely.

We must all be careful what we think of ourselves. Our heavenly Father is no respecter of man and the self-righteous works of human beings do not impress Him either. This should act as a prompter for us to be humble before God almighty. Our confidence in God grows through a fruitful personal relationship with Him—a growing relationship with God at the centre of all things. We all need to undertake continuous self-assessments to ensure we are on the right track.

> *So, if you think you are standing firm,*
> *be careful that you don't fall!*
> *—1 Corinthians 10:12*

There is always room for improvement in your life, so don't get comfortable in your past achievements or with your present endeavours.

✪Selective Christianity✪

There is a tendency for "selective Christianity" in today's world, to only embrace what we like from the Bible and leave the rest. Some churches avoid talking about "social sins" or areas of the Bible that are unpopular, such as treating people as inferior, prejudice, underpaying workers, racism and more. Luke 3:11–14 identifies some of the kinds of changes we ought to make when we adopt a new life in Christ. It said the man who has two tunics should share with someone who has none, tax collectors should not collect more taxes than is legal and soldiers should not extort money or accuse people falsely, but must be content with what they receive from their employers.

We are at times too busy judging and condemning others while we ourselves are guilty of wrongdoing in the eyes of God. Being a Christian and an obedient child of God is not limited to when we are in church or among fellow Christians. It must become a lifestyle that the world can see. It's not only when we carry a Bible or wear a cross or dog collar that people should identify us as Christian. The world should be able to see from our actions that our identity is truly in Christ, even without bumper stickers or preaching directly.

Thus, by their fruit you will recognise them.
—Matthew 7:20

A person I once knew who happened to be a Christian told me he got along with almost everyone, but he couldn't stand Somalians. The Bible does not teach us to be selective in those we like. Biblical principles should supersede any cultural beliefs because the Bible has absolute authority over all things. We must be careful in a world where moral values are continually being reshaped by popular views, political correctness, and liberalism. Many Christian leaders are careful to avoid biblical teachings that clash with cultural principles, moral values, or popular opinions of the day, which means some Christians may grow up (in Christ) knowing only a selected truth about the Word of God. Our master Himself had to contend with people not liking what He preached. Sometimes, His teachings drove people away, but He never compromised or adjusted what He said to please anybody.

> *On hearing it, many of his disciples said, "This is a hard teaching. Who can accept it?"*
> —John 6:60

I spoke to a pastor recently who preached about sin and judgment day. After the service, a member of the congregation said to him, "Haven't we heard enough of this hell fire and brimstone preaching?" The truth is, like the teaching in John 6:25–60, some preaching makes many people uncomfortable, but does that mean they should not hear it?

Because we are being convicted through the Holy Spirit, the flesh wants us to put up a "barrier" to defend its territory (to stop us from changing our ways for the better). In John 6:60–70, Jesus didn't soften or water down His teachings when he realized most of his followers did not like what he was teaching. Rather, he proceeded by expanding further on the truth which many didn't like, so some deserted him. This did not stop him or affect his ministry. He even challenged the twelve disciples to leave with the rest if they were so inclined.

This passage demonstrates a clear example of what we should do when we have been given a clear mandate from God to deliver a message to His people, even if the message is unpopular. Jesus did not try to please man by being "economical" or "diplomatic" with the truth, so why should we be influenced by the desire to please man? The Bible warned that there would be a time when people would select pastors and teachers who preached what is "politically correct," what sounds good to them, teachings that don't upset them and teachings that fail to convict them of the truth.

> *For the time will come when men will not put up with sound doctrine. Instead, to suit their own desires, they will gather around them a great number of teachers to say what their itching ears want to hear. They will turn their ears away from the truth and turn aside to myths.*
> —2 Timothy 4:3–4

When we look around the world today, we see a significant growth in new age religions, some of which are being incorporated into teachings in some churches. Many of the teachings sound good to the ears, but they are not from God (though they may refer to God in their teachings). We must bear in mind that Satan knows the Bible very well and he will come in different shapes and forms to try to lead the children of God astray. He quoted verses from the Old Testament (in Matthew 4) to Jesus in his attempts to lure Jesus into sin, and today he is still very much active. This is why we are encouraged to watch and pray, and pray continuously.

Another area some Christians often avoid in the Bible is the book of Revelation and topics to do with judgment. We certainly will not be able to claim ignorance - of not knowing what the Bible says, because the Bible is there for all to read - not just pastors or only in the church. We mustn't avoid "difficult topics" that make us uncomfortable. I will encourage everyone to also read the Bible independently of what is taught in churches, Bible studies and study guides. You should begin with prayer, asking God to speak to you through whatever passage you read. If you read and don't understand, then stand on the following verse:

> *If any of you lacks wisdom, he should ask God, who gives generously to all without finding fault, and it will be given to him.*
> —James 1:5

This verse doesn't say God gives wisdom only to special people, but highlights its availability to all without fault. If we seek God diligently, and ask Him with an open mind, he we make wisdom available to us; wisdom to understand the word of God.

We must avoid falling into the "I am safe," "I've got heaven secured," "This is for sinners," or "This is for baby Christians" trap. The Bible states,

> *"Not everyone who says to me, 'Lord, Lord', will enter the kingdom of heaven, but only he who does the will of my Father who is in heaven. Many will say to me on that day, 'Lord, Lord, did we not prophesy in your name and in your name drive out demons and perform many miracles?' Then I will tell them plainly, 'I never knew you. Away from me, you evildoers!'"*
> —Matthew 7:21–23

This passage speaks to all. We cannot serve God, and persist in our sinful ways, just because the world doesn't see what we do in secret. Some of us hold prominent positions, yet engage in ungodly activities both in secret and public, thinking we've gotten heaven covered because of the capacity we serve in. An important fact we fail to remember is that God is not a "respecter of man". He will use who He pleases to achieve His work irrespective of whether we live a holy life or not. Being endowed with the ability to perform miracles for example, does not give liberty to exploit this ability for personal gain or commit other acts of sin. God is not accountable to anyone and you cannot expect to enter the kingdom of heaven if you have lived a sinful life.

A preacher of many years, who started on the right track but lost his way, may still possess the ability to minister and perform miracles for two reasons. Firstly, he can preach based on experience and techniques acquired over the years (preaching the Word of God through the flesh rather than through the Spirit of God), supported by the trust that has been built up with the congregation. Secondly, the faith of the believer heals and not the faith of a minister. A pastor could pray and fast for healing for a person but if this person doesn't believe he can be healed, the pastor would be wasting his time. Now if this person believes he will be healed, his faith will act as the catalyst for receiving healing though the minister may have lost his way (or is engaging knowingly in sinful acts). A number of times in the bible, Jesus testified to this truth that the faith of the one who desires healing makes them well (Mark 10:52, Like 7:50, Mark 5:34, Luke 17:19). The pastor doesn't do the healing, but God is the only one who effects the healing. The minister is a medium (channel) for the healing. Hence all glory must go to God (the Source). Matthew 7:21-23 should be a wake-up call for us all not to assume we are guaranteed the Kingdom of Heaven just because we prophesy, cast out demons, perform miracles or write Christian books.

He who has ears, let him hear.
—Matthew 11:15

How do we know the will of God as highlighted in verse 21 of Matthew 7? We ascertain God's will via personal relationship with Him, reading the Bible, making time to listen to God (being quiet in the presence of the Almighty), not forsaking the gathering of the children of God, loving God with all of our heart and soul, and loving our neighbours as ourselves. The ability to discern doesn't come overnight. It is acquired through discipline, focus on God, shunning distractions and allocating more time during the day to meticulously seek the Almighty.

✪

Our righteousness is like filthy rags before God (Isaiah 64:6) and we cannot attain God's righteousness through bribing Him or serving Him, because He knows our hearts and thoughts and the motives behind what we do. Self-righteousness (or religious/legalistic approach) is operating through the flesh. Living a God-centred, righteous life and changing your ways cannot be done in the flesh. If you attempt it this way, you will change some things, struggle with some and completely fail with others. Why? Because the flesh is naturally engineered to sin post-garden of Eden (Adamic nature).

What is the solution? How do you ensure success in changing your ways?

By living through the Spirit!

> *It is because of him that you are in Christ Jesus, who has become for us wisdom from God—that is, our righteousness, holiness and redemption.*
> —1 Corinthians 1:30

There is no need for self-righteousness. Man-made righteousness involves operating through the flesh, and changing your ways can certainly not be done in the flesh. You have already been made righteous through Christ Jesus according to the passage above. This righteousness is manifested by living through the Spirit. Your flesh cannot be under complete control of the Spirit of God if you keep operating in the flesh. You must operate through the Spirit, allowing the Holy Spirit to be the driver of all daily decisions.

When you become born again, you are born of the Spirit (John 3:5–8), and for this reason, you should live through the Spirit. Note that verse 8 of John 3 highlights the fact that you need not think or know what is going to happen but just go with the "flow of the Spirit." I am still learning, because doubts and worries still try to creep in now and again, but God is great and He is in control.

Yes, God gave us knowledge, free will and all that we need for victorious living, but how are we faring? Constant worry, rushing everywhere, not enough time in the day, lack of contentment, numerous disappointments and more characterise the lives of many. Then there is the issue of grading sins like a bit of stealing, cheating and evading a bit of tax, or judging others and many more wrongdoings all because we choose to live through the flesh. But in the Spirit of God, we have wisdom, righteousness, holiness and redemption (1 Corinthians 1:30). Living through the Spirit will facilitate the demonstration of the fruits of the

Spirit. If we try to demonstrate these fruits—love, joy, peace, patience, kindness, goodness, self-control, faithfulness and gentleness (Galatians 5:22–23)—through the flesh, we are likely to struggle and fail. (I've tried to do it in the flesh and failed terribly! But through the help of the Holy Spirit, I am now having more success stories). We can successfully exhibit these fruits by living through the Spirit and keeping in step with the Holy Spirit of God.

Since we live by the Spirit, let us
keep in step with the Spirit.
—Galatians 5:25

Chapter 3

Priorities

So we've looked into the need to change and know that it is not about us but all about Jesus. So what should our priority be if it is not about us?

Romans 12:1–2

Mathew 6:25–34

Colossians 2:8

Hebrews 13:6

Romans 12:1-2 encourages us not to conform any longer to the standards of this world but focus on renewing our minds. This is done through reading the Bible, having a proper personal relationship with God (where He speaks to us and we listen as well as talking to God in prayer), attending the gathering of the children of God and any godly activities that develop the impact of the Holy Spirit of God in us. We then focus our efforts on carrying out the instructions in Matthew 6:33.

Our most important priority is to seek the kingdom of God and His righteousness. The kingdom is God's governing influence here on earth, and righteousness is being in right standing with God. Therefore, we should not be taken captive through hollow and deceptive philosophies that are built on human traditions (Colossians 2:8). We certainly have nothing to be afraid of, because the Lord is our helper (Hebrews 13:6).

✪The Breakdown✪

> *But seek first his Kingdom and his righteousness, and all these things will be given to you as well.*
> —Matthew 6:33

Where is God's kingdom? God has a kingdom in heaven where He reigns supreme. His desire to expand His kingdom led to the creation story and man being the governor. Let us imagine the old British Empire when Britain sought expansion around the world. In each of the colonies, a governor was installed, who is answerable to the monarch and ruled on his or her behalf. In a similar way, God expanded His domain from the heavenly realms to the earth and gave man charge of it just like the British did with governors (Genesis 1:26). However, unlike the British with a kingdom (empire) that existed physically on Land, God's kingdom is in the heart of men. He exists in Spirit, and those who worship Him must worship in spirit and truth (John 4:24). In order for God to fully manifest His existence in our hearts, we must purify ourselves and offer our bodies as a temple of the Lord God almighty (Romans 12:1). When we truly feel the presence of God continually in our lives, His desires becomes ours, we become light to the world by living a life pleasing to Him and attracting more people to the Kingdom of light naturally. Therefore, we as children of God must seek to expand God's influence here on earth. He lives within us and it is His desire for all men to know Him and gain eternal life. We all have a role to fulfil in the expansion of the Kingdom of God. Our role as part of the body of Christ, working for the expansion of God's kingdom through the spreading of the gospel, is dependent on our calling (1 Corinthians 12:28-31). Some are called to be pastors, teachers, musicians, accountants, lawyers, pilots and so on. Whatever we are called to do, let us do it for Christ. Our calling is discussed in more detail later on.

> *Then Jesus came to them and said, "All authority in heaven and on earth has been given to me. Therefore go and make disciple of all nations,*

> *baptising them in the name of the Father and of the Son and of the Holy Spirit, and teaching them to obey everything I have commanded you. And surely I am with you always, to the very end of the age."*
> —Matthew 28:18–20

In the above passage, Jesus confirms the desire of God to expand His domain (reign) here on earth by commanding us to make disciples for Him. Before we can make disciples for Christ, we must become disciples ourselves. Being a disciple for Christ Jesus involves, give up the desires of the flesh and putting God first. It also involves dedicating ourselves to meticulously studying the Word of God, gain knowledge and understanding of his Word, and applying it in our daily living. This is arguably one of the most difficult things to do. I personally struggle with putting God first with daily battles of responding to the desires of the world such as my career, business, exams and other things that seem so important today but amount to nothing in the context of eternal life. Sometimes we deceive ourselves by saying we are doing it for God but deep in our hearts, we know they are being done to gratify the desires of the flesh. We are encouraged by the bible not to give up because God is our helper and he will help us to change our priority to the expansion of God's kingdom here on earth. This is what seeking first the kingdom of God means.

Righteousness involves being in right standing with God as previously stated. An integral aspect of being in right standing with God is clearly outlined in the first part of Hebrews 11:6. It says, *"And without faith it is impossible to please God."* I could effectively give my money to charities, help the needy, sing in church, read my Bible, and do many more wonderful things, but without faith they are worthless. Faith and love underpin our relationship with God. In the first place, faith is a prerequisite for accepting Jesus Christ as our Lord and Saviour. Think about it. Did you see Jesus in the flesh before accepting Him as your Lord and saviour? Most definitely not! Therefore, it was through faith that we all accepted Him as Lord. So anyone who says they don't have faith just didn't realise it was faith in the first instance they exercised to become a follower of Christ. But how does faith tie into righteousness as was stipulated in the first line of this paragraph?

Now when a man works, his wages are not credited to him as a gift, but as an obligation. However, to the man who does not work but trust God who justifies the wicked, his faith is credited as righteousness.
—Romans 4:4–5

Righteousness cannot be earned through the works of man (Romans 3:20). We are made righteous through Christ Jesus (1 Corinthians 1:30). Living by the principles of righteousness through Christ Jesus encapsulates the theme of faith. In other words, acknowledging we are nothing and we can do nothing in our strength without Jesus in addition to choosing to have complete trust in God for all things, signify faith in Him. This faith is credited as righteousness in the sight of God. This is why the bible encourages us to humble ourselves before God (James 4:10), something I struggle with on many occasions. The freewill bestowed upon us leads us to thinking we accomplish things in our strength; failing to admit that only God makes all things possible. He is Omni-present, and nothing happens without the awareness of God.

So, faith goes hand in hand with righteousness, and we cannot be in right standing with Him without faith. Therefore, Matthew 6:33 and Matthew 28:18–20 should be verses that drive us in our daily living.

When should I change?

> *Another disciple said to him, "Lord, first let me go and bury my father." But Jesus told him, "Follow me, and let the dead bury their own dead."*
> —Matthew 8:21–22

We sometimes fill our lives with excuses for not doing the will of God or not doing more for God: "When I get married …" "When I finish my studies …" "When I become a pastor …" "When I have my kids …" "When my kids are grown …" "When I retire …" "When I get promoted …" "When I change jobs …" Many of these excuses originate from Satan because it is not in his best interest that we are all fully committed to Christ. It's bad for his business, so he will find numerous ways of occupying the lives of the children of God, making them "too busy for God".

Some of us get complacent, comparing ourselves with others. A person could say, "I already work as a Sunday school teacher" or "I am the treasurer of my local church," and think that's all that God requires of them. I can honestly say that my top priority has not always been God. But He is changing me and as each day passes and I am getting better through Christ Jesus strengthening me.

The time to change our "Number 1" priority to seeking the expansion of God's kingdom is now. God is very patient, but His patience is not limitless. He sends us little reminders; calling us, encouraging us and more. We must promptly respond to His call and change as we would have no excuse on judgement day. For many reading this book, (just like it was for me) this is another wake-up call from God about what your main concern should be. You must draw nearer to Him in personal relationship so you can ascertain His calling for you, His plan and will for your life (if you are unaware of His plans for you).

How do I change my priorities?

1. *"You shall have no other gods before me"* (Exodus 20:3).

Many of us have little gods that eat into valuable time that could have been spent developing a fruitful relationship with our God and responding effectively to Matthew 6:33. These gods include, but are not limited to: television, video games, mobile phones, the Internet, friends, hobbies, computers, social media, ambition, food, career and sleep. Now, these things are not necessarily bad. In fact, God can use any of these mediums or persons to communicate with us. But if we aren't watchful and prayerful, Satan can use all of these as instruments of distraction from God. Rather than exercise control over them, they exert control over us, inevitably becoming little gods in our lives.

I have heard some people say that they can't live without something (usually a perishable object or comfort of some sort), but God almighty is the only one that we should categorically say we cannot live without. When we have God, understand the love He has for us, forge a committed personal relationship with Him and obey His commands, then we will realise that with Him on our side, we have everything.

2. Life through the Spirit.

Those who live according to the sinful nature have their minds set on what that nature desires; but those who live in accordance with the Spirit have their minds set on what the Spirit desires. The mind of a sinful man is death, but the mind controlled by the Spirit is life and peace; ...
—Romans 8:5–6

'Sinful nature' refers to what the flesh wants. The flesh wants all the things that provide "temporary pleasure." Excesses of the things listed in the paragraph above are what the flesh desires. However, if we set our minds on things of the Spirit, then the influence of the Holy Spirit increases in our lives.

What are the things the Spirit desires that we can set our minds on? The things the Spirit desires are worshiping God; loving our neighbours; reading the Word of God, meditating on it and putting it into practice daily. It is also of great importance to speak in tongues (where possible and appropriate), interpret as often as we can, pray without ceasing, and not forsake the gathering of the children of God.

For anyone who speaks in a tongue does not speak to men but to God. Indeed, no-one understands him; he utters mysteries with his spirit.
—1 Corinthians 14:2

He who speaks in a tongue edifies himself, but he who prophesies edifies the church.
—1 Corinthians 14:4

For this reason anyone who speaks in a tongue should pray that he may interpret what he says.
—1 Corinthians 14:13

Pray continually.
—1 Thessalonians 5:17

> *Let us not give up meeting together, as some are in the habit of doing, but let us encourage one another—and all the more as you see the Day approaching.*
> —Hebrews 10:25

3. Doing the Word of God.

> *But the one who received the seed that fell on good soil is the man who hears the word and understands it. He produces a crop, yielding a hundred, sixty or thirty times what was sown.*
> —Matthew 13:23

The parable of the sower (Matthew 13:1–23) talks about various types of Christians, but the only type God wants us to be is like the seeds that fell on good soil. It's no good hearing the Word on Sunday and at Christian gatherings, but not putting it into practice. Drawing nearer to God in a personal relationship will provide a sustainable platform for us to increase the influence of God in our lives and live a fruitful life.

Many of us want to live fruitful lives, but we often complicate our lives by having too many things going on and Jesus not being the central focus.

> *See to it that no one takes you captive through hollow and deceptive philosophy, which depends on human tradition and basic principles of this world rather than on Christ.*
> —Colossians 2:8

Now is the time to desire to be free from earthly principles and connect fully to Christ! Let us gear our efforts to being set free from this bondage and allow the Holy Spirit to make Christ a permanent and prominent fixture in our lives.

But what if I don't change my priorities?

> "...You have rejected me", declares the LORD. "You keep on backsliding. So I will lay hands on you and destroy you; I can no longer show compassion on you..."
> —Jeremiah 15:6

God is a very patient and loving God. He is also a just God. We know the truth; hence, we cannot claim ignorance. We all need help changing our priorities and maintaining focus on Christ Jesus. The starting point is to surrender all to God with the next logical step being prayer. You can ask a friend or your partner to support you in prayer as you begin the journey of changing your priorities and living through the Spirit. Don't wait till you finish university, change jobs, get married, retire, finish your exams, have more money, have more time, or have any other excuse. Today, right now, is the perfect time to make a fresh commitment to Christ and ask Him to help you remain steadfast.

Please take a moment now to pray before you proceed.

Chapter 4

The Change

"Not by might nor by power, but by my Spirit," says the LORD ALMIGHTY.
—Zechariah 4:6

Changing our priorities involves living through the Spirit of God. Living through the Spirit is a common theme in this book. This is because many of us do not live life through the Holy Spirit; we therefore find it difficult to overcome the sinful nature. We struggle with sin and the desires of this world. The flesh is weak, but the Spirit of God has life eternal.

I can do everything through him who gives me strength.
—Philippians 4:13

The key in the passage above is "him." "Him" here represents Jesus, and he is the bedrock and foundation that all things need to be built on. The next thing to look at is "everything." There is always a danger of misquoting the Word of God, and this verse is certainly a candidate. We'd be wasting our time trying to apply this verse to a plan that isn't sanctioned by God. Whatever we ask or hope for must glorify the name of our heavenly Father for it to come under the "everything" umbrella.

If you remain in me and my words remain in you, ask whatever you wish, and it will be given you. This is to my Father's glory, that you bear much fruit, showing yourselves to be my disciples.
—John 15:7–8

Verse 8 of John 15 qualifies the "everything" in Philippians 4:13. The things we wish for must be things that glorify the name of God and help us to be fruitful disciples of His. If they do not meet these criteria, we would be wasting our time and energy in prayer. Now God sees our hearts, so if I pray for money and say to God, "Oh, I will use it to build schools and churches" but deep down I am seeking the money to glorify myself, then that prayer will almost certainly not be answered. This is because God sees my motive behind the prayer and probably because He loves me and doesn't want me to end up down the wrong path. So I probably won't receive answers to that prayer for my own good.

> *When you ask, you do not receive, because you ask with wrong motives, that you may spend what you get on your pleasures.*
> —James 4:3

Humility before the God of heavens and earth will help a lot in our prayers. Take a look at these verses:

> *A man with leprosy came and knelt before him and said, "Lord, if you are willing, you can make me clean." Jesus reached out his hand and touched the man. "I am willing," he said. "Be clean!" Immediately he was cured of his leprosy.*
> —Matthew 8:2–3

What I want to focus on in the text above is "Lord, if you are willing." The man here recognised that ultimately all decisions belong to God. Rather than force his healing to happen, he asked for the will of God to be done. Even when Jesus was in the garden of Gethsemane, He prayed God would take away His cross but ended with "may your will be done." This is how we should end all our prayers to God. If Jesus Himself can pray like that, then I believe we ought to follow in our Master's footsteps. The Lord's Prayer has a line that goes, "Your will be done on earth as it is in heaven," which highlights the need to end or begin our prayers with God's will being done.

✪Life through the Spirit Revisited✪

Let's return to living life through the Spirit, which is a very important aspect of our living. Our change starts from saying "No" to sinful nature and its desires. These are things that are contrary to what the Spirit wants, and a number of them are listed in Galatians.

> *The acts of the sinful nature are obvious: sexual immorality, impurity and debauchery; idolatry and witchcraft; hatred, discord, jealousy, fits of rage, selfish ambitions, dissensions, factions and envy; drunkenness, orgies and the like. I warn you, as I did before, that those who live like this will not inherit the Kingdom of God.*
> —Galatians 5:19–21

Sinful nature is not limited only to the above but includes anything that is not of God, does not glorify God and is not in accordance with what the bible instructs us to do. Idolatry today includes obsession with one's looks, weight, and image; spending countless "unproductive" hours on social networking sites; too much time in front of the TV; obsession with food, cars, clothes and other material things. Basically, anything that consumes a great deal of our time and passion (including sleep) should be reviewed with spiritual principles applied to it.

Now that we are aware of the things we should avoid and manage better, we can explore what has been made available to us when we live through the Spirit. These things are called the "fruits of the Spirit."

> *But the fruit of the Spirit is love, joy, peace, patience, kindness, goodness, faithfulness, gentleness and self-control. Against such things there is no law.*
> —Galatians 5:22–23

By examining our lives, seeking to rid ourselves of the sinful nature through the help of Jesus and living through the Spirit, we can reallocate our time productively. You'd be amazed how much extra time you have in your life by limiting the desires of this world. We can refocus our energy on seeking God in personal daily relationships, growing the Spirit man, communicating with God throughout the day and engaging in fruitful activities.

If need be, take a moment to ask God to change your desires from the sinful nature to the things of the Spirit of God.

One must bear in mind that change may not happen overnight. We need to be persistent in prayer. Luke 18:1–8 tells the story of a woman who persisted in her plea with a judge for justice against her adversary. The judge eventually gave in to her; hence, we must adopt similar principles of perseverance in prayer to effect the change in our ways.

A very effective acronym in persistence with God is PUSH, which stands for "Pray until something happens." The Bible also encourages us not to give up. In essence, it depends on how much we want the change that will (to a large extent) determine how successful we are. Take a little child, for example, on a hot Saturday afternoon. The child knows there is ice cream available, that child will not give up until he/she gets it. In a similar fashion, we must continually call on God about our desired change until it happens.

Once the change commences, it becomes a natural occurrence that God becomes first in our lives. When we genuinely put God first, He has a vested interest in us. It is important we succeed in God's business; therefore, He will automatically provide everything we *need* without asking (Matthew 6:33). Note the emphasis on "need." There is a clear difference between "need" and "want," but in today's world, that difference is somewhat opaque.

Let us debug ourselves from the way the world classifies "need" today, because some of the luxuries we have often engulf us in "the comfort-zone captivity." Colossians 2:8 encourages us not be held captive by the deceptive philosophy of this world.

The change enables us to lead productive lives that produce fruit in all seasons.

Blessed is the man who does not walk in the counsel of the wicked or stand in the way of sinners or sit in the seat of mockers. But his delight is the law

> *of the* L ORD *, and on his law he meditates day and night. He is like a tree planted by streams of water, which yields its fruit in season and whose leaf does not wither. Whatever he does prospers.*
> —Psalm 1:1–3

We are all capable of bearing fruit in all seasons, if we have the right priorities, change our ways and utilise our talents to glorify God. He is capable of taking our gifts away from us and giving them to someone who will put them to better use like in the parable of the talents (Matthew 25:14–30). If we let Him, He will purify us by helping us to remove all hindrances to spiritual growth in our lives and amplifying our good attributes for His glory.

> *He cuts off every branch in me that bears no fruit, while every branch that does bear fruit He prunes so that it will be even more fruitful.*
> —John 15:2

If we let Him, He will cut off every unproductive branch in our lives. He has a purpose for each of us here on earth, and as we draw nearer to Him through personal relationship, it becomes clearer which part we play in His kingdom.

Let us continually seek the Lord diligently on our journeys to eternity with Christ.

Chapter 5

Comfort-Zone Christians

Whoever finds his life will lose it, and whoever loses his life for my sake will find it.
—Matthew 10:39

A reason why some Christians aren't growing is because they are enjoying the "comfort zone." In the comfort-zone trap, there is little emphasis on spiritual growth but a big focus on earthly comforts, such as bigger houses, nicer cars, bigger salaries and other such earthly things. There is no talk about carrying our crosses (Matthew 10:38), making disciples of nations (Matthew 28:19), storing up riches in heaven (Matthew 6:19–20) and putting God first (Matthew 6:33).

Sometimes, we think we are already doing our bit because we attend church regularly, pay our tithes, and maybe even already function as a pastor, treasurer, musician, or Sunday school worker and think complacently that we've secured eternity. But the Bible says,

> *So, if you think you are standing firm,*
> *be careful that you don't fall!*
> *—1 Corinthians 10:12*

Some may believe that there is no need to grow spiritually, that once saved and not doing "very bad things" you'll be okay and you can maintain the status quo as long as you confess your sins. In truth, nobody stays the same; you either increase or decrease. Of course, it is possible not to be aware of any change within a short time frame, but it becomes more evident over the medium to long term that you have either increased or decreased. This goes for our walk with Christ.

> *When I was a child, I talked like a child, I thought*
> *like a child, I reasoned like a child. When I became*
> *a man, I put childish ways behind me.*
> *—1 Corinthians 13:11*

> *In fact, though by this time you ought to be teachers,*
> *you need someone to teach you the elementary truths*
> *of God's word all over again. You need milk, not solid*
> *food! Anyone who lives on milk, being still an infant, is not*

acquainted with the teaching about righteousness. But solid food is for the mature, who by constant use have trained themselves to distinguish good from evil. Therefore let us leave the elementary teachings about Christ and go on to maturity, not laying again the foundation of repentance from acts that lead to death, and of faith in God, instruction about baptisms, the laying on of hands, the resurrection of the dead, and eternal judgment.
—Hebrews 5:12-6:2

Amazing, isn't it? During Paul's time, there were serious concerns about the lack of spiritual growth of Christians and I believe this problem is widespread in churches across the world today. In education, we all started at the beginning but did not remain there; primary, secondary, maybe university for some and for others, higher education. Many of us are in jobs or further education as a result of progress in the past. Can we say the same of our walk with Christ? Are you a baby in Christ? Have you grown spiritually since you've been saved? Are you born again in Christ?

Some will say they've been born again or been Christians for ten, twenty, or more years, but they haven't grown spiritually. We cannot keep drinking "breast milk" at the age of ten or fifteen years in Christ, lacking understanding of elementary teachings mentioned in Hebrews 6:1–2. As we develop in Christ, there should come a time when teaching on these elementary subjects becomes insufficient, just as we wouldn't expect a person in secondary school that has been learning for over six years to still be learning basic arithmetic, such as 1+1. A time should come when a person desires to know more about God, taking the sermon in the church and meditating upon it at home.

A burning desire to increase spiritually should drive us out of our "comfort zone." Our personal relationship should become our primary source of receiving from God as we develop our Spirit man with other sources complementing it. This should spur us to do more for Christ.

What do I get from a relationship that is not available in a religion?

The ability to test in private what you've heard or received from various sources is an important feature of relationship with God.

> *Dear friends, do not believe every spirit, but test the spirits to see whether they are from God, because many false prophets have gone out into the world.*
> —1 John 4:1

This was true of the old times and is very much true today. There are many false prophets clothed in sheep's wool, and unless we test the spirit, we cannot be certain what we hear is from God. Indeed, what you are reading here right now must be tested to ensure it is truly the word from God. But how can you test or know for certain that what you are hearing is real without a sound relationship with your maker? This is certainly an important reason why we all must seek to grow continually in Christ.

Many Christians desire to grow in Christ but are unwilling to make the necessary sacrifice, the sacrifice of developing a personal time of worship and communion with God because we are too busy for God and comfortable with our relationship with Christ. Sometimes, because we know the Bible, we feel we will be okay. But do we understand what the Bible says? Do we practice what we learn? Do we obey the instructions given by Christ Jesus?

...my people are destroyed from lack of knowledge.
—Hosea 4:6

He replied, "The knowledge of the secrets of the kingdom of heaven has been given to you, but not to them."
—Matthew 13:11

For this people's heart has become calloused; they hardly hear with their ears, and they have closed their eyes. Otherwise they might see with their eyes, hear with their ears, understand with their hearts and turn, and I would heal them.
—Matthew 13:15

A lot of Christians attend churches and places of worship regularly but still do not get the message of Christ. They hear the Word of God, but it does not take root. God does wonders in their lives, but they cannot perceive the works of God in their lives. They read the Word of God but lack understanding. This is because they do not have the knowledge of the secrets of the kingdom of heaven.

The Jews during the time of Jesus thought the messiah was to come and rescue them from the rule of the Romans and other enemies. In other words, they were expecting a political messiah; a war leader. Today many Christians are seeking the messiah for earthly prosperity and political deliverance. But Jesus is here for eternal life, to save our souls not our bodies, to free us from spiritual captivity, not physical liberation and to help us amass wealth in heaven and not on earth.

Let's take a look at the "Jesus model." His life here on earth sets a good example for us to emulate. He did not have riches or assets. He went around helping the needy, using the power bestowed on Him. So why are we failing to walk in His footsteps? Why are we chasing promotion at work, our own business, more houses, bigger houses, better holidays, more gadgets and all the things that will be destroyed along with the old earth when the new one is being formed? It's because hearts have been "calloused" (Matthew 13:15). Hearts of Christians have been "hardened" not to be able to truly hear the Word of God. The ability to understand the Word is nonexistent; hence, though people may have given their lives to Christ by being born again, some are still under a form of bondage. Hearts have been pre-programmed to function in a certain way, to have similar aspirations and worries of "pagans" (Matthew 6:32).

Chapter 6

The Call

*But if serving the L*ORD *seems undesirable to you, then choose for yourselves this day whom you will serve, whether the gods your forefathers served beyond the River, or the gods of the Amorites, in whose land you are living. But as for me and my household, we will serve the L*ORD.
—Joshua 24:15

What is God calling you to do today? Are you on the right path?

The answers to these questions can be obtained from a profound personal relationship with our maker with a desire to break free from the "comfort zone." The Bible says the Lord rewards those who attentively seek Him (Hebrews 11:6). You cannot find out God's will for your life in a quick one-minute prayer early in the morning or late at night with no other contact with God throughout the day. People that genuinely hear from God and prophesy didn't receive that ability by spending little or no time in personal relationship with God. It takes discipline, good time management and help from the Holy Spirit to allow quality time for communicating with God not just once but throughout the day.

The things that are stopping us from communing properly with God and responding in obedience to His Word will not be so important on the last day, so let's reconsider the value we place on the things of this world.

> *For we brought nothing into the world,*
> *and we can take nothing out of it.*
> —1 Timothy 6:7

That's correct! We cannot take any of our riches, certifications, degree programmes, fame or connections out of the world. Once our bodies die, those things also die to us; however, the riches stored up in heaven don't die, so why don't we focus more effort on storing up riches in heaven? The same death that awaits a poor man awaits a rich man! This simple logic is known to Christians, yet many fail to act appropriately on this reasoning. Why? What's stopping us?

God has a calling for each of us. He marks out a road for us to achieve His purpose—some for noble use; others for common, everyday use (Romans 9:21). Some people are on the right path; some are trying to find it. And some are completely on the wrong path. He is the potter and we are the clay. We cannot run from Him or hide from Him.

> *Nothing in all creation is hidden from God's sight. Everything is uncovered and laid bare before the eyes of him to whom we must give account.*
> —Hebrews 4:13

> *"Can anyone hide in secret places so that I cannot see him?" declares the LORD. "Do not I fill heaven and earth?" declares the LORD.*
> —Jeremiah 23:24

God has a particular purpose He desires to achieve through our lives. Though we may try to run away or occupy ourselves with other things, if He wills, He will make us do it.

> *But the LORD provided a great fish to swallow Jonah, and Jonah was inside the fish three days and three nights.*
> —Jonah 1:17

Has God called you to do something and you keep postponing it? Are you chasing selfish ambitions? Is God in what you are doing? Do you have peace that passes all human understanding? Are you like the people in Haggai

1:2? Let us re-examine our lives, reorder our priorities, and ask where God is in what we are doing. If you carry on in the direction God isn't in, then destruction lies ahead. Don't, because you have your mind set on doing or not doing something, cause others around you to suffer like Jonah did. It is not about you but all about Him.

> *Here I am! I stand at the door and knock. If anyone hears my voice and opens the door, I will come in and eat with him, and He with me.*
> —Revelation 3:20.

> *Now to each one the manifestation of the Spirit is given for the common good. To one there is given through the Spirit the message of wisdom, to another the message of knowledge by means of the same Spirit, to another faith by the same Spirit, to another gifts of healing by that one Spirit, to another miraculous powers, to another prophecy, to another distinguishing between spirits, to another speaking in different kinds of tongues and to still another the interpretation of tongues. All these are the work of one and the same Spirit, and he gives them to each one, just as he determines.*
> —1 Corinthians 12:7–11

Sometimes, we are ready to commit ourselves in service to God but then become selective of what we want to do for Him. A common mistake that many of us make when serving God is that we'd like to choose what we do for God, usually something convenient that fits into our already established lifestyle or something that makes us feel important in the sight of man. But that's not the way it works with God. It's His business, therefore His choice which part we play in the body of Christ.

It's like seeing a job advert for a full time human resources assistant, applying for the job and telling the business owner, "No, I don't want to do human resources for you, but I want to be director of finance and I'll come into work when I feel like." A number of Christians sometimes force their way into key jobs in the church/kingdom of God (knowing it's the wrong job), undertake duties poorly with fickle commitment, then hold on to it with a tight grip, preventing others (who are capable of doing a much better job) the opportunity to assume responsibility for the position.

There are many things we can do for God, many things we can be, many things we can give, but nothing is better than to simply *obey*.

We must bear in mind that when it comes to serving in the kingdom of God, it's not about what we want to do or where we want to be seen functioning. Rather, it should be all about God and what He wants us to do. We certainly cannot find out His will for our lives without dedicating adequate time to studying the Word of God - meditating on it, hearing from God and praying. We must come to the presence of God with a completely open mind to enable us to trust in God and obey what He asks us to do. Whatever God wants us to do, He has made provision for all eventualities; therefore, all we need do is to trust and obey.

When God gives us a job to do, we can stand on His Word knowing He will provide wisdom, knowledge, and boldness to undertake the work proficiently, even if we don't have previous experience or know what to do. The Holy Spirit knows what to do, and He also promised not to leave or forsake us.

> *Never will I leave you; never will I forsake you.*
> *—Hebrews 13:5*

Our ultimate calling is to bring "good news" to all. What part we play in this bigger picture will often depend upon our skills and how God wants to use it for His glory. Sometimes, the comfort we derive from worldly pleasures hinders us from doing the work of God properly. We mustn't get comfortable with this world, because this world in its present form will not exist post-second coming of Christ. We should be focused on the new earth, as this will last a lot longer than the present earth (Revelation 21:1, Isaiah 65:17, Isaiah 66:22, and 2 Peter 3:13).

Let us seek the face of the Lord to establish His will for our lives rather than go for the most "prestigious" jobs in the kingdom of God, which may not be what He wants us to do. The bible says that we must be the servant of all to be great in God's kingdom

The verses below should serve as an encouragement for those in the "comfort zone" and those that need to answer to "the call." Anyone can be in the comfort zone, irrespective of whether you are serving God at present or not. Ask God in prayer to guide you as you read the following verses and help you make necessary changes.

He who is not with me is against me, and He who does not gather with me scatters.
—Matthew 12:30

… And anyone who does not take his cross and follow me is not worthy of me.
—Matthew 10:38

Whoever finds his life will lose it, and whoever loses his life for my sake will find it.[1]
—Matthew 10:39

'No servant is greater than his master.' If they persecuted me, they will persecute you also. If they obeyed my teaching, they will obey yours also. They will treat you this way because of my name, for they do not know the One who sent me.
—John 15:20–21

---

[1] Losing one's life in this passage means dying to self (desires) and putting God's desire first.

Consider it pure joy, my brothers, whenever you face trials of many kinds, because you know that the testing of your faith develops perseverance. Perseverance must finish its work so that you may be mature and complete, not lacking anything.
—James 1:2–4

Do not love the world or anything in the world. If anyone loves the world, the love of the Father is not in him. For everything in the world—cravings of sinful man, the lust of his eyes and the boasting of what He has and does—comes not from the Father but from the world. The world and its desires pass away, but the man who does the will of God lives forever.
—1 John 2:15–17

Therefore, since we are surrounded by such a great cloud of witnesses, let us throw off everything that hinders and the sin that so easily entangles, and let us run with perseverance the race marked out for us.
—Hebrews 12:1

Do not be misled: "Bad Company corrupts good character."
—1 Corinthians 15:33

If any of you lacks wisdom, he should ask God, who gives generously to all without finding fault, and it will be given to him. But when he asks, he must believe

> *and not doubt, because he who doubts is like a wave of the sea, blown and tossed by the wind.*
> —James 1:5–6

Doubt is a reason why many prayers go unanswered. It is a big area many Christians are struggling with, but there is help at hand. When we struggle with doubt, we should simply ask God for help with our doubt (unbelief). In Mark 9, a man brought his son to Jesus because the boy had an evil spirit. In verse 24, the man confessed he needed help to overcome his "unbelief" (doubt that Jesus could heal his son). He got the help he needed, overcame his unbelief and his son was healed. In essence, when we have doubts, we should just ask God to help us overcome our doubts in a simple prayer, so we can proceed with our main prayers and receive answers to them.

We all need to draw nearer to God in relationship, irrespective of the stage in our walk with Christ. Those still in the "comfort zone" need to wake up from "spiritual slumber." God is a just God. He makes the rules, and we cannot bend the rules to suit ourselves. We cannot pick and choose the bits of the Bible we like and ignore the bits we don't like. We can't just read and claim Deuteronomy 28:1–14 but conveniently ignore, avoid, or skip verses 15–68. There are blessings (rewards) for obedience and consequences (punishment) for disobedience. Hence, obedience to God includes (but is not limited to) paying our tithes, even when it seems difficult or impossible (Malachi 3:8–10), not forsaking the gathering of the children of God (Hebrews 10:25), making disciples of all nations (Matthew 28:19–20), loving our enemies and praying for those who persecute us (Matthew 5:44), putting God first before all things (Matthew 6:33), giving thanks in all situations, even when things seem very bad (1 Thessalonians 5:18) and all the other instructions that seem somewhat difficult to put into practice all the time.

Chapter 7

Struggling With Sin

For sin shall not be your master, because you are not under law, but under grace.
—Romans 6:14

Sin can be uncomfortable when people point out the sins we engage in on a daily basis. We try to justify it by admitting we are human beings, however, we are quick to point out the sins of others.

'Why do you look at the speck of sawdust in your brother's eye and pay no attention to the plank in your own eye? How can you say to your brother, "Let me take the speck out of your eye," when all the time there

> *is a plank in your own eye? You hypocrite, first take the plank out of your own eye, and then you will see clearly to remove the speck from your brother's eye*
> —Matthew 7: 3–5

We take a higher moral ground in justifying how bad the wrong-doings of others are. We condemn and judge others whilst we are also engaged in sinful activities. We have accepted and re-conditioned our body to live with our daily sins, sometimes with no desire to change. But this is not right in the sight of God. We must look to our heavenly father for assistance in living a sin-free life.

On the other hand, sin prevents Christians from having a sound relationship with God. We are sometimes scared to come to God or feel we are not worthy of coming to His presence because of our past or current sins. But the Bible says there is no condemnation for those who are in Christ Jesus (Romans 8:1).

> *Let us then approach the throne of grace with confidence, so that we may receive mercy and find grace to help us in our time of need.*
> —Hebrews 4:16

> *...but because Jesus lives forever, he has a permanent priesthood. Therefore he is able to save completely those who come to God through him, because he always lives to intercede for them.*
> —Hebrews 7:24–25

✪Condemnation✪

Hebrews 4:16 makes additional provision for us when we feel like condemning ourselves excessively or think that God cannot forgive us for a particular sin. There was a particular time when I felt God warning me of an impending sin, to watch, pray and be prepared. I took it onboard, or at least I thought I had it covered, but went in unprepared. I came out falling prey to what I had been warned about. I felt so condemned that, for at least a day, I did not feel worthy of communicating with God. I proceeded to fasting for a few days because I felt so ashamed, since I'd been warned and hadn't made adequate preparations, such as praying in the spirit, drawing nearer to God in worship, etc. I condemned myself to the point of questioning if God would forgive me.

But He forgave me because of Hebrews 4:16 and Romans 8:1. I was reminded there is no need to condemn myself, because I am already in Christ Jesus. I was also prompted that I can approach the throne of grace with confidence to obtain mercy that I needed because Jesus (our high priest) is continually interceding on my behalf. Romans 8:34 and Hebrews 7:25 testify to the fact Jesus is there interceding for us on the right hand of God.

Now that took a huge weight of my mind when I received those words and read the relevant passages. I was set free from the spirit of despair and condemnation. Nobody needs to condemn themselves for sins past or present, thereby blocking a potentially fruitful relationship with the Father.

Let go and let God.

✪Continuous struggle with sin✪

In Romans 7:14–24, Paul talks about struggling with sin. He elaborated that he knew the good he should do but found it impossible to do the good. However, the bad things he shouldn't do were the things he found easier to do and he kept doing them.

This is true about many of us as we struggle with sin. We talked about changing our ways in chapter 2, but in practice, some of these things seem impossible to change permanently, like Paul found in Romans 7. He noted in verse 18 that no good lives in him; however he directed this bad attribute to his sinful nature. He talked about a desire from his innermost self to delight in God, do His will, and be obedient to Him.

A lot of us share this desire of wanting to please God but see another law at work in our bodies: the cravens of the sinful nature, the desire to blend in and please the world we live in, the desire for acceptance by the world, greed, selfishness and personal enrichment, the desire to be heard, the desire to be important, jealousy, envy, covetousness, pride, boasting, self-gratification, earthly obsession, expansion and improvement of earthly comfort, the desire to take the easy route in life, the difficulty in staying on the straight and narrow path and so on. Wow! Sounds like we are slaves to sin and the following comments become justifiable when committing sin:

> Oh, we are only human.
>
> We have the grace of God.
>
> God will understand.
>
> He is a merciful God.
>
> I am born again, so all is well.
>
> It is impossible to live here on earth without compromise.
>
> As long as I confess my sins every day, then it's all good.
>
> There's nothing we can do.
>
> My sin is not as bad as the sin of politicians, prisoners, and celebrities.
>
> Who cares anyways? You only live once.
>
> I attend church regularly and serve God.
>
> Everyone is doing it, so what hope do we have?

Since the pastor and vicars are doing it, it must be okay.

I am not hurting anybody.

I am surrounded by sinners, so I don't have much of a choice.

It's my job and I have no choice but to do it, else I'd lose my livelihood.

I do it to protect my family.

This is the only way to get ahead of the game.

Surely, even the Pope sins.

Nobody is perfect, and if anybody were, they would be in heaven.

I've tried, failed, and given up, so I accept my fate.

You can't take the Bible too seriously.

Things are not like in the Bible times anymore. Things are different now.

I speak in tongues.

The Bible needs to adapt to the changing times.

No one can see me.

Hey, come on. At least we aren't the ones that crucified Jesus.

I am very religious.

I can do what I like in my house.

I give a lot of money to charity.

I don't know where to go or where to turn for help, so I do what I have to do.

I am merely withholding the truth.

The spirit is willing, but the flesh is weak.

God doesn't love me.

He gave us free will.

Though the works of my hands are questionable, I help a lot of people, so they kind of cancel each other out.

I perform miracles, so it must be okay with God.

Occupational hazard.

However, the Bible says,

> *For the wages of sin is death, but the gift of God is eternal life in Christ Jesus our Lord.*
> *—Romans 6:23*

> *The fear of the* LORD *is the beginning of knowledge,*
> *but fools despise wisdom and discipline.*
> —Proverbs 1:7

I don't believe we fear (revere or respect) God enough and this is why many of us keep committing the same sin and repenting over and over again. The respect we have for God is sometimes reflected in praying in our beds and falling asleep while praying or during prayer, thinking of a million other things or being distracted with things like mobile phones and plans for the next day. If we can't revere Him during prayer or personal devotions, how can we revere Him (by living a sin-free life) in our daily living?

A lot of us find it easier to obey the laws of man (e.g., pay your taxes or don't break into other people's houses) because there are immediate consequences for disobedience. But many take for granted the Law of God—probably because we can't see God and punishment is not until judgement day in many circumstances.

For example, the Bible says we should not judge, but we at times find it difficult not judging politicians for their actions/inactions, footballers, bankers and personalities on TV, even in light-hearted discussions and jokes. Even if their actions are wrong, is it our place to judge?

> *You, therefore, have no excuse, you who pass judgment*
> *on someone else, for at whatever point you judge*

> *the other, you are condemning yourself, because you who pass judgment do the same things.*
> —Romans 2:1

Ignorance, lack of understanding, lack of willingness to change, or bondage of some sort will cause a person to ignore the guidance from the Scriptures and persist in living differently from what the Bible says; using any number of excuses such as the ones listed above as a reason. Take the example of a boy who beats his little sister up. His parent tells him off and tells him not to do it again. The boy proceeds to apologise to his father but continues this pattern day after day. When the parent questions the child, asking why he keeps persisting in beating his little sister, would the parent accept the statement, "Oh, I'm only human," or any of the other excuses? Probably not. So why should we think it is okay to carry on living a life of sin and expect God to be accepting of our wrongdoings despite the fact that we have been delivered from the bondage of sin through the blood of Christ? If we keep living a life of sin, then we are living non-victorious lives. We wouldn't accept if a thief keeps breaking into our houses and keeps apologizing would we? Just like stealing is a sin, all sins before God are equally unacceptable. Now these words are not designed to condemn anyone. On the contrary, they are written to encourage us. God disciplines those He loves.

It is because of God's love that I was prompted to change my way, reminded of the promises for living an obedient life and led to passages in the Bible that highlight consequences for disobedience. I am by no means the finished article, but through the help of God, I am getting better on a daily basis.

> *For the wages of sin is death, but the gift of God is eternal life in Christ Jesus our Lord.*
> —Romans 6:23

> *But the cowardly, the unbelieving, the vile, the murderers, the sexually immoral, those who practise magic arts, the idolaters, and all liars—their place will be in the fiery lake of burning sulphur. This is the second death.*
> —Revelation 21:8

We all have a unique opportunity to repent and turn from our sinful ways for good. Our attitudes toward sin must change, and we must quit "decriminalising" certain sins. No need to take a higher moral ground. We need to humble ourselves before God and accept that sin is sin before the Almighty. The only sin that carries more weight than others is a sin against the Holy Spirit.

> *I tell you the truth, all the sins and blasphemies of men will be forgiven them. But whoever blasphemes against the Holy Spirit will never be forgiven; he is guilty of an eternal sin.*
> —Mark 3:28–29

The Bible encourages us to continuously watch and pray so we don't fall into temptation. Praying continuously is not limited to once or twice a day but progressively throughout the day. Being in constant communion with Christ can mean we have even hundred prayers in one day made up of a mixture of short prayers (with as little as four words) and long prayers.

Watch and pray so that you will not fall into temptation.
The spirit is willing but the body is weak.
—Matthew 26:41

Pray continually.
—1 Thessalonians 5:17

Praying continually is a paramount act for combating the "spiritual pull" of temptation while enabling us to draw nearer to God. One prayer is not enough to guide us through the course of a twenty-four hour period. This is why we are encouraged to watch and pray all the time, as the Devil is always on the prowl. We must develop a praying habit if we are to overcome the plans of the Evil One.

I have hidden your word in my heart
that I might not sin against you.
—Psalm 119:11

Chapter 8

Not All Battles Are Physical

*For our struggle is not against flesh and blood,
but against the rulers, against the authorities,
against the powers of this dark world and against
spiritual forces of evil in the heavenly realms.*
—Ephesians 6:12

A lot of times, we think the things we struggle with are physical whereas many are spiritual battles. As God is drawing many people into the kingdom of light, Satan is also at work trying to tempt people into the kingdom of darkness. A forwarded e-mail/text I received a while ago had content similar to this: (It was an extract from a discussion between Satan and his cohorts).

"Hmm, let us fill the life of Christians with so much junk that they won't have time for their God. Let us give them more responsibilities at work, so they will come back home too tired to read their Bibles or share the Word of God with their families. Let's give them more functions, parties, friends and activities that have nothing to do with God, to keep them busy and stop them thinking about God. Let us give them ambition that is not of God, so that they won't be able to do God's will. Let us keep them hooked up on TV, games, the Internet and other things that gratify their fleshly desires, spending their time wastefully to prevent them from seeking God in personal relationships, Bible study and other godly activities. Let us give them the spirit of fear to prevent them from witnessing to others about Christ (sharing the good news); in fact, let us make them ashamed of being Christians in their work places, schools, gyms and everywhere possible. Let us give them progress in earthly things to stop them from thinking about progressing spiritually. Let's give them a materialistic spirit, so that they will focus on acquiring earthly possessions at the expense of storing up riches in heaven. Let us give them a spirit of complacency, so they will not feel the need to grow in Christ."

As illustrated above, it's not in the best interest of Satan and his crew that we remain children of God and as we seek Him more or attempt to draw closer to Him, Satan would obviously tries to stop this by distracting us or trying to fill our time with worthless engagements. When you are too busy for God, who do you think is happier: God or Satan?

Spiritual battles are not limited to demons and dark powers only. Satan can come in any form. He could come in the form of a promotion at work that would take you away from God and your family, money that would lead you to committing all kinds of sin, friendships that lead down the crooked path and even as a false prophet.

Watch out for false prophets. They come to you in sheep's clothing, but inwardly, they are ferocious wolves.
—Matthew 7:15

The Devil is called the deceiver for a reason. When he comes to the children of God, he rarely comes dressed in red with horns, looking like an ugly beast. He comes in temptations of various forms, using earthly things that the flesh desires. Jesus experienced this firsthand (Matthew 4:1–11). For this reason, it is of great importance we pray continually and ask God (our all-knowing Father) to guide our decision making.

The Devil tempts us with various tricks to separate us from the love of God. God cannot behold sin and sin can cause a significant hindrance to the growth of our relationship with Christ. But note this: God's love for us is unconditional. He loves us irrespective of the sins we've committed in the past.

If we are ready to repent and genuinely willing to change, He will accept us and help us. Nothing can separate us from the love God has for us.

> *Who shall separate us from the love of Christ? Shall trouble or hardship or persecution or famine or nakedness or danger or sword? As it is written: "For your sake we face death all day long; we are considered as sheep to be slaughtered." No, in all these things we are more than conquerors through him who loved us. For I am convinced that neither death nor life, neither angels nor demons, neither the present nor the future nor any powers, neither height nor depth, nor anything else in all creation, will be able to separate us from the love of God that is in Christ Jesus our Lord.*
> —Romans 8:35–39

Given the fact that we are more than conquerors and Christ has delivered us from the bondage of sin, why are we still living sinful lives? Why are we still struggling with sin?

This is because we have not fully set our minds on what the spirit desires. We've set our minds on what the sinful nature desires (the things of this world), with God secondary in our lives (after we've done everything and if there is a bit of space then we can squeeze Him in). Because the impact of our conscience is weak, we've conformed to the standards of this world and have been ignoring the voice of God.

> *Those who live according to the sinful nature have their minds set on what that nature desires: but those who live in accordance with the spirit have their minds set on what the spirit desires. The mind of sinful man is death, but the mind controlled by the Spirit is life and peace; the sinful mind[2] is hostile to God. It does not submit to God's law, nor can it do so. Those controlled by the sinful nature cannot please God.*
> —Romans 8:5–8

If we don't feed our spirit man adequately, its influence will wither with the flesh taking dominance. Just like food. If you don't eat enough food, the body will gradually diminish. The same is said of the influence of the Spirit of God within us, as we cannot live through the Spirit if we've set our minds on what the flesh wants: money, fame, acceptance, self-gratification, etc. Our minds cannot remain void either. They (our minds) have priorities as to what the flesh desires or what the Holy Spirit of God desires. This is why there is so much sin around. One can't say, "I don't read my Bible and I don't believe in God, but I don't sin and am a good person," because there isn't an in-between. You are either for Christ or against Christ.

> *He who is not with me is against me, and he who does not gather with me scatters.*
> —Matthew 12:30

---

[2] In the NIV translation, the sinful mind is the mind set on desires of the flesh.

The only way we can win the spiritual battle is have the whole "Armour of God" (Ephesians 6:10–18) on at all times to defend us from the various schemes of the Devil. These are schemes that try to take our minds away from what the Spirit of God desires and prevent us from living victorious lives. We must equip ourselves with the belt of truth, gospel of peace, shield of faith, breastplate of righteousness, helmet of salvation, and sword of the spirit (which is God's Word). It is therefore essential we know the Word of God and have it at hand, ready to defend ourselves from the plan of the Evil One.

My wife and I started getting up very early in the mornings to pray recently. On this particular day, a family that we were very close to in the recent past came to my wife's mind. We were fully aware that the Devil had been tormenting this family for a period of time, based on stories the couple had shared with us. They moved away from the area and we were unable to reach them on the telephone numbers they provided. So my wife decided to pray for them. Immediately after the prayer, she got attacked with a headache that felt like a piercing from her right eye straight through the brain. The pain was immense, intense, persistent and somewhat unbearable. We knew it was a result of us taking the time to offer prayer for this couple.

We prayed and prayed, but the headaches did not abate. We were very concerned and the thought of rushing to the hospital started filtering in. But we recognised our identity in Christ, reminded God of His promises and exercised our faith in the name of Christ. She received healing that very day and Satan was defeated. A few days later, I wanted to pray (during my own personal prayer time) for the same couple, but thoughts of what had happened to my wife came to me. I was hearing thoughts saying, *Are you sure you really want to pray for these people? You do realise that if you get attacked, you won't be able to go to work and you've only just started at your new place of work. It won't look good on your record. You'd better wait till Friday, so that if you fall ill, then you can have Saturday and Sunday to rest.*

Through the power of God, I rebuked Satan, reminded him he had been defeated already by Jesus on the cross, and went about my prayers. Nothing happened to me that day by the special grace of God.

Satan and his forces are always roaming about, looking for people to devour. It is therefore of utmost importance that we pray continually in the spirit. The idea of "comfort-zone," laziness and complacency is not of God. These things prevent us from increasing in Christ; therefore, we must not allow them to creep into our lives. If they are in our lives, we must rid ourselves of them immediately through the use of the full "Armour of God."

The more we set our minds on what the Spirit of God wants, the more we give control of the flesh to the Spirit of God.

Chapter 9

Encouragement and Conclusion

✪**Ambassadors of Christ**✪

> *In the same way, let your light shine before men, that they may see your good deeds and praise your Father in heaven.*
> —Matthew 5:16

Unless our lives are actively geared to increase in Christ on a daily basis, we will continually struggle with sin and the spiritual battles. Do you remember in an earlier chapter where we discussed declassification (grading) of sin by many? Well, that doesn't work with God. We can't "pull the wool" over the eyes of the all-knowing God who knows our thoughts even before we have them. A life geared for Christ is not about being a perfectionist; rather, it's about living a godly life.

> *Therefore, brothers, since we have confidence to enter the Most Holy Place by the blood of Jesus, by a new and living way opened for us through the curtain, that is, his body, and since we have a great priest over the house of God, let us draw near to God with a sincere heart in full assurance of faith, having our hearts sprinkled to cleanse us from a guilty conscience and having our bodies washed with pure water.*
> —Hebrews 10:19–22

> *Therefore since we are surrounded by such a great cloud of witnesses, let us throw off everything that hinders and the sin that easily entangles, and let us run with perseverance the race marked out for us.*
> —Hebrews 12:1

Firstly, as Christians, we are ambassadors of Christ. Non-Christians and young Christians see us. Therefore, what we do, say and how we live our lives will have a great impact on the perception of what others think of us as children of God. Many Christians have driven away (knowingly or unknowingly) other Christians from God through acts of hypocrisy and sin. A person I was sharing the Word of God with recently refused to go to church because of hypocritical acts of his work colleagues who are Christians. His Christian colleagues invited him to church and emphasised the need to go to church but their actions at work were not actions one would associate with Christians. He said one of them was a Sunday school teacher or pastor yet fiddled the books at work regularly.

Others have been prevented from becoming believers as a result of our actions or the way we live as Christians. I once heard a story that Mahatma Gandhi was exiled to Kenya during the struggle for independence from British rule. In his time in East Africa, he read the whole Holy Bible and developed a desire to know more. He attended a church run by some Americans, but he was turned away because he wasn't white. He then proceeded to state, "I would have been a Christian if I hadn't met one." This story was apparently confirmed by one of Gandhi's adopted sons. I am not sharing this story to put anyone down but rather to alert us that we are capable of turning people away from Christ as a result of our actions. Gandhi may have led a whole nation to Christ if he had been welcomed into that church. That person we could have spoken to about Jesus or been Christ's ambassadors in front of may have become an integral part of the body of Christ. Let us live as true ambassadors of Christ.

Secondly, we all have a race (path) marked out for us. As discussed earlier, it's not about us or what we think. Rather, it's all about Him. Hebrews 12:1 points out the fact that we all have a path marked out for us. Let us propose in our hearts to find out what path is marked out for us and get on it quickly. All the money and achievements in this world will not matter on the last day. God is not impressed by bank balances and PhDs. It's our hearts that He looks at, so let's get our priorities right.

✪Grace Covers Sin✪

What shall we say then? Shall we go on sinning, so that grace may increase? By no means! We died to sin; how can we live in it any longer?
—Romans 6:1–2

There is the school of thought that many hold onto which proposes that once a person is saved, you have grace and it covers you for all sin so you don't have to worry. I certainly believe that grace has been provided us by God but does not serve as a liberty to carry on sinning. The Bible says God cannot behold sin, so how can we carry on living a sinful life and expect God to be okay with it? Of course, God is merciful, loving, kind and patient, but He is also just. The Bible says God will carry out His judgement on man with speed and finality (Romans 9:28). It makes sense for us to recondition our hearts and minds to get rid of sin, making changes by getting rid of those things that hinder and the sin that entangles (Hebrews 12:1), by asking God to help us.

In the same way, count yourselves dead to sin but alive to God in Christ Jesus. Therefore do not let sin reign in your mortal body so that you obey its evil desires.
—Romans 6:11–12

For sin shall not be your master, because you are not under law, but under grace.
—Romans 6:14

Grace should be utilised to set us free from the claws of sin rather than trap us in a lifestyle that leads to death. In Romans 3, Paul writes that no one is righteous, because the righteousness of man is like filthy rags before God. However, we are made righteous through faith (v. 22) and not through the works of our hand or obeying the laws of God. Romans 3:31 then concludes that although we are made righteous through faith in Christ, we must not nullify the law. That is, we must not say, "We are Christians, so whatever happens, we will make heaven." But He encourages us in the last part of verse 31 that we must uphold the law of God; the Ten Commandments are summarised into loving God with all of our hearts and soul and loving our neighbours as ourselves.

Nothing stays empty. Even a closed container with no contents will have air in it. In the same way, we cannot purge ourselves of sin and think we can keep it out without filling the space with something fruitful. Therefore, we must become "slaves" to obeying the Word of God. Some may say, "I don't think it's right to be a 'slave' to obeying the Word of God. After all, He gave us freewill." However, if we aren't slaves to obeying the Word of God (righteousness), we will become slaves to sin.

> *Don't you know that when you offer yourselves to someone to obey him as slaves, you are slaves to the one whom you obey—whether you are slaves to sin, which leads to death or to obedience which leads to righteousness?*
> —Romans 6:16

> *You have been set free from sin and have become slaves to righteousness. I put this in human terms because you are weak in your natural selves. Just as you used to offer the parts of your body in slavery to impurity and to ever-increasing wickedness, so now offer them in slavery to righteousness leading to holiness.*
> —Romans 6:18–19

Like the Bible says, no one can serve two masters (Matthew 6:24). We are either slaves to righteousness (obedience to the Word of God) or slaves to sin. There isn't an in-between or a third option and I am sure we all know which leads to eternal life.

When things are good, we are happy to do things or exist without God, but when things start going wrong or we hit a dead end, we are ready to give up our freewill for God to help us. We can't pick and choose when we want Him. Either we are fully committed to God or not. We will certainly do a lot better and make fewer mistakes with God in the driving seat.

Conclusion

We need God in our lives more than we anticipate, and it's a shame many of us "use" God. Of course He loves us unconditionally and He will always listen to us because we are His children and He provides our needs. But He also has His own desires that only we can meet. He desires a relationship with us, where we put Him first and this is well documented across the Bible. However, a lot of us have little or no personal relationship with Him. Some of us have a "take-take" relationship where all we do is ask and seldom give to Him. Imagine yourself having a relationship with someone and he or she calls only to get something from you. I don't think anyone would like a one-way relationship where the other party is there for what he/she can get out of the relationship. We call these kinds of people "opportunists."

Yet, we also, could be described as opportunists many a time in our relationship with God. Desperation makes us realise we need God more than we thought and sometimes it's too late. It is not too late to seek God now while He may be found. Tomorrow may be too late. Let us agree to develop our relationship with God (irrespective of how good or bad our present one is with Him), giving Him the honour He deserves.

> *Seek the L*ORD *while he may be found;*
> *call on him while he is near.*
> —Isaiah 55:6

Humble yourselves before the Lord, and he will lift you up.
—James 4:10

Made in the USA
Columbia, SC
06 June 2024